A celebration of WINTER in rhyme

Mariana Books Rhyming Series Book 4 Seasons

Challenge: Find the stanza that doesn't rhyme.

By
Roger Carlson

When the last leaf falls,
and the last tree goes bare;
there's no doubt about it
winter is in the air.

The days become shorter,
while the nights grow long;
the temperature slowly drops,
and the snow starts falling strong.

The last season of the year
is the coldest one too;
the warm colors of autumn,
turn to white, grey, and blue.

3

As the snow falls thicker,
it covers the paths and streets well;
it's time for the first step
do you know it? Can you tell?

It's time for cozy winter clothes
so have a good look around;
once you're covered from head to toe,
you're ready to hit the ground.

Put on warm, snug sweaters
warm long fluffy scarves too;
don't forget socks, boots, gloves and hats,
that's all you have to do.

If you're still feeling cold,
add some layers before you go;
your fluffiest jacket or warmest coat,
and then you can play in the snow.

Everywhere you look it's white,
there's snow as far as you can see;
soft, powdery, clean, white snow,
waiting to become whatever you want it to be.

So many choices,
but where do you start?
What can you build this winter,
that will set it apart?

Perhaps a giant snowman
with a long carrot nose?
Start by rolling a giant snowball,
and you'll see how it goes.

Next, you make a second one
and stack it on your first big ball;
but wait, you're not done yet,
make one final ball that's all.

Now place the final ball on top,
and it becomes the head;
you just made a giant snowman.
What should we name him... Fred?

Begin decorating the snowman,
starting with the side;
Take two long, thin branches
From the ground, that are dried.

Now Fred's arms are done,
but his neck still looks too cold;
grab a scarf to make him warm,
now he looks quite bold.

To make his pointy nose,
a long orange carrot should do;
use Mom's big buttons for his eyes,
and small ones for his smile too.

Put a pipe in Fred's mouth,
and add a top hat that's black;
your giant snowman is ready
to shield you from any attack.

You can hide behind Fred,
and throw as many snowballs as you can;
take aim and hit the most targets,
that's the only snowball fight plan.

Or you could lay on the ground,
and stretch your body wide;
to make beautiful snow angels,
before you have to go inside.

Winter is the coldest season,
but Mom's kitchen warms the mood;
it smells amazing and delicious,
because it's full of home-cooked food.

Winter is the time to eat
hot soups and spicy chili,
gooey pasta and roasted veggies,
creamy potatoes, toasty tomatoes or cheesy broccoli.

But there's something more exciting,
than winter games and food;
it starts with "S" and ends with "A"
and he's a big old jolly dude.

Winter also means Christmas time,
the best holiday all year;
Christmas means lots of presents,
love, laughter, family time, and cheer.

Merry
Christmas

When autumn is done and winter starts,
go find the best fir tree;
cut it down and bring it home,
and set it up in place of the TV.

Now it's time to decorate,
dig out the Christmas lights;
unravel them, put them on,
and let them shine so bright.

Now get the ornaments,
bells, balls, candy canes, and tinsel
in gold, silver, red, blue and green,
drape them around your tree well.

Next hang the stockings,
one for you, your siblings, Mom, and Dad;
hang them on the fireplace,
now, what else is there to add?

26

We need treats for Santa!
Milk and cookies as a prize,
to thank him for your gifts,
before he goes back to the skies.

Christmas morning is the best,
all the gifts beneath the tree!
When you rip off the paper,
so excited by what you see.

28

Winter is the last season,
but it has the most good cheer;
goodbye, farewell, take care,
we'll see you again next year!

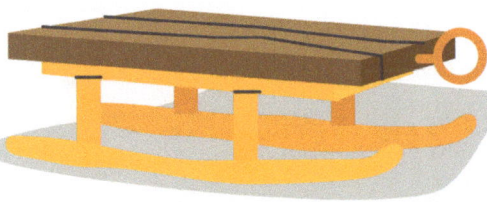

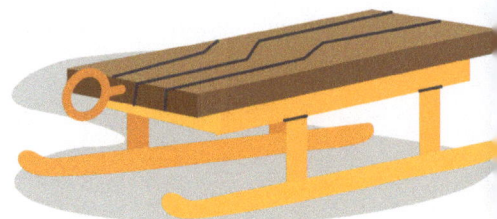

Find these and all of the other Mariana Publishing books for sale on Amazon and our web site
www.marianapublishing.com

WAYBACK BOOKS

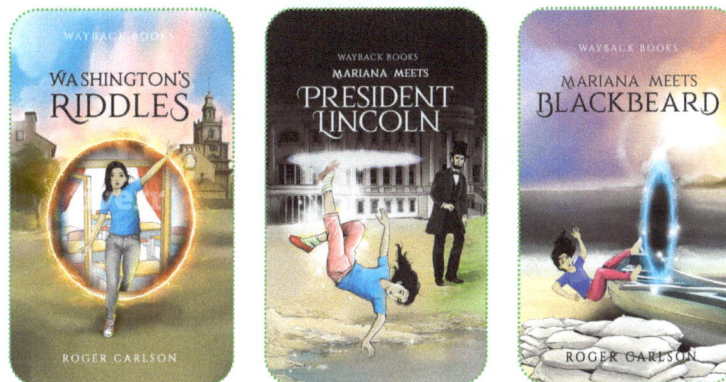

Find us on:

f @marianapublishing   @marianapublishing   @LlcMariana   Mariana Publishing Online

Copyright © 2020 by Roger Carlson

All rights reserved, including the right of reporduction in whole or in part in any form. This book or any portion thereof may not be reproduced or used in any manner whatsoever without the express written permission of the publisher except for the use of brief excerpts for review purposes.

ISBN: 978-1-64510-045-4 (Hardback)
ISBN: 978-1-64510-044-7 (Amazon Paperback)
ISBN: 978-1-64510-046-1 (Print On Demand)

www.ingramcontent.com/pod-product-compliance
Lightning Source LLC
Chambersburg PA
CBHW061050090426
42740CB00002B/109

9 781645 100447